EASY PIANO SOLO

CHRISTMAS HITS

T0081653

ISBN-13: 978-1-4234-3178-7
ISBN-10: 1-4234-3178-2

HAL•LEONARD®
CORPORATION
7777 W. BLUEMOUND RD. P.O. BOX 13819 MILWAUKEE, WI 53213

Visit Hal Leonard Online at
www.halleonard.com

CONTENTS

BLUE CHRISTMAS

Words and Music by BILLY HAYES
and JAY JOHNSON

Moderately, with feeling

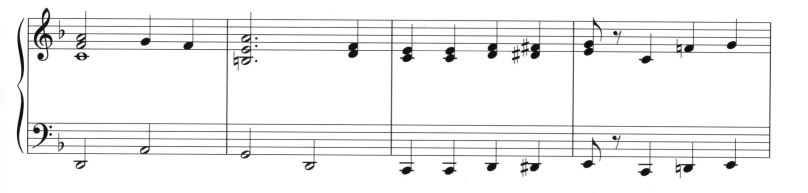

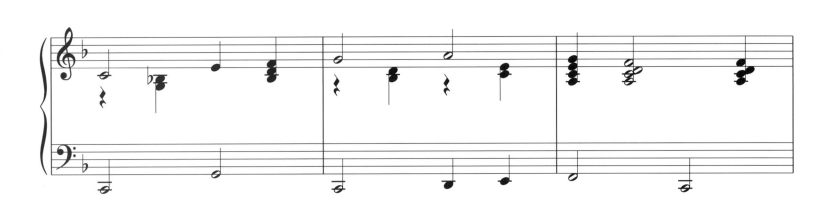

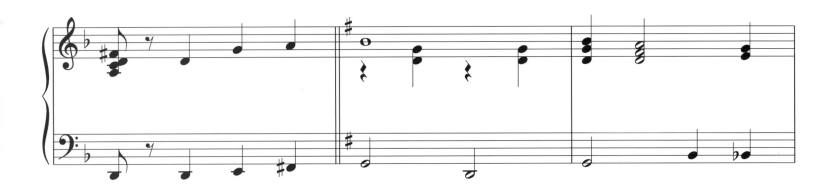

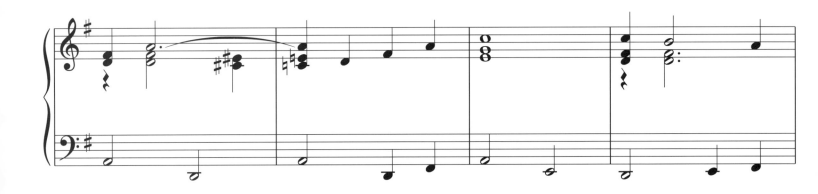

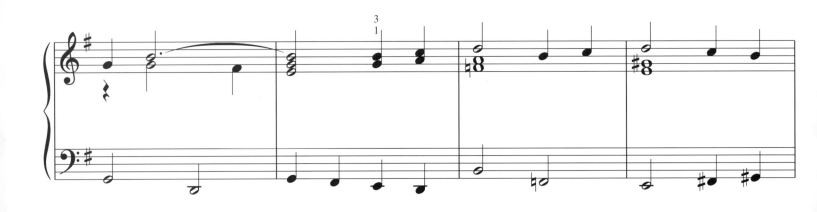

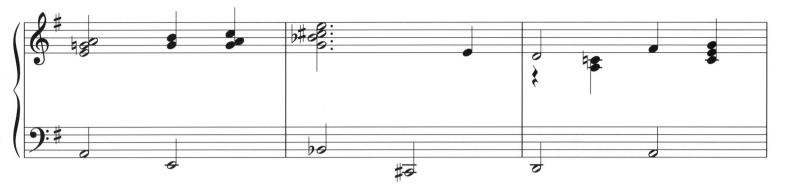

THE CHIPMUNK SONG

Words and Music by
ROSS BAGDASARIAN

Bright, humorous

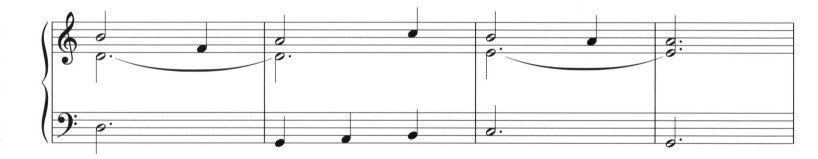

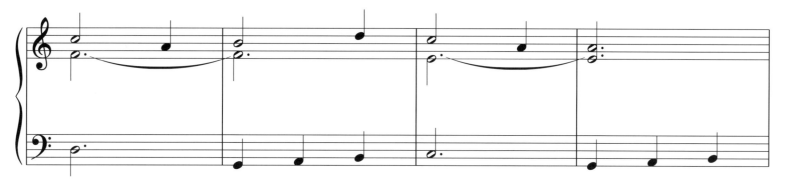

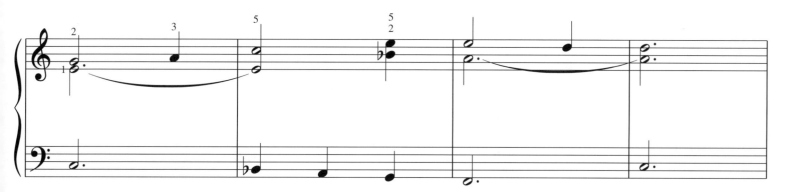

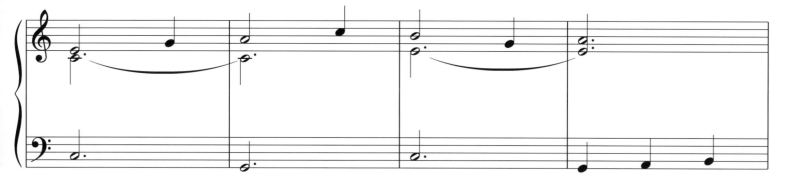

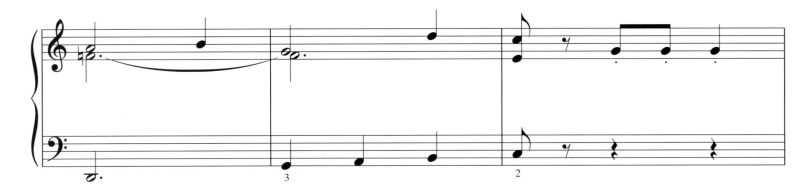

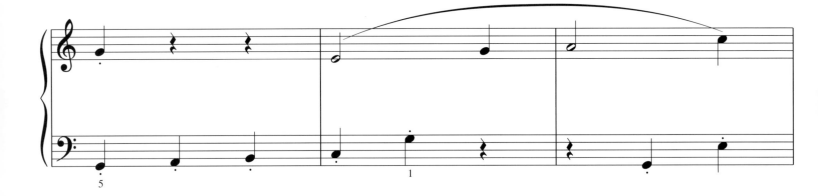

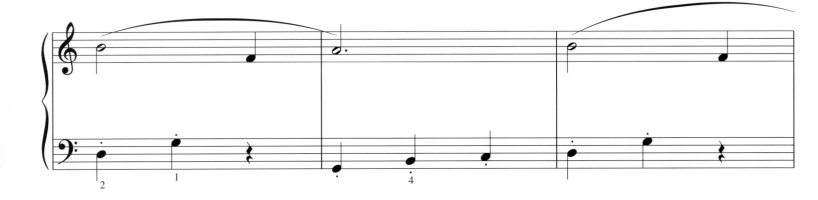

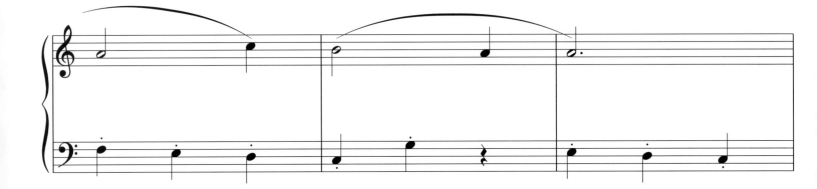

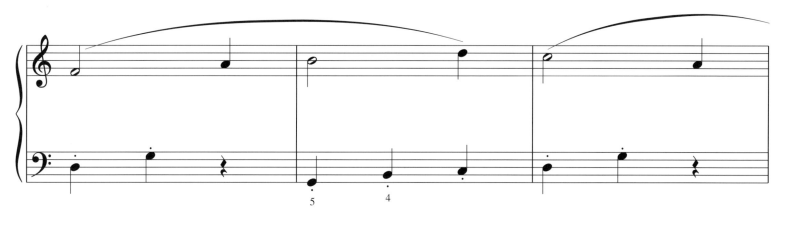

5   4

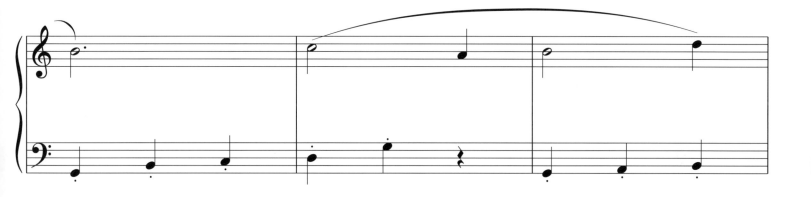

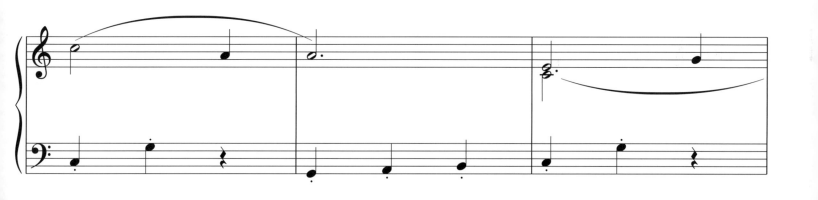

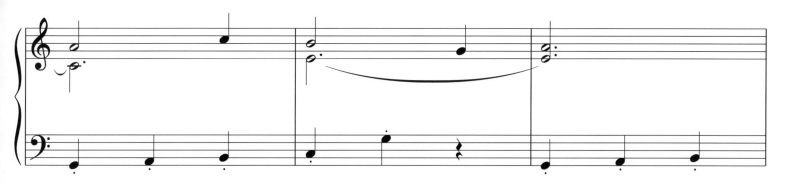

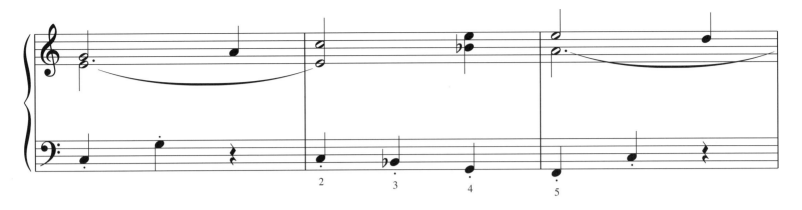

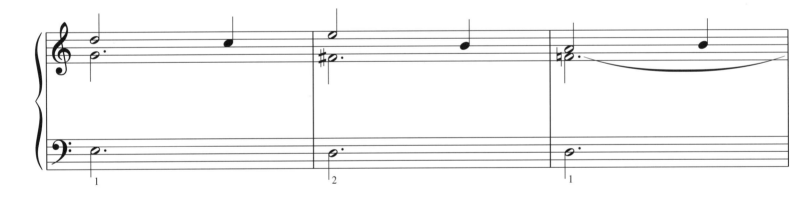

FELIZ NAVIDAD

Music and Lyrics by
JOSÉ FELICIANO

Moderately

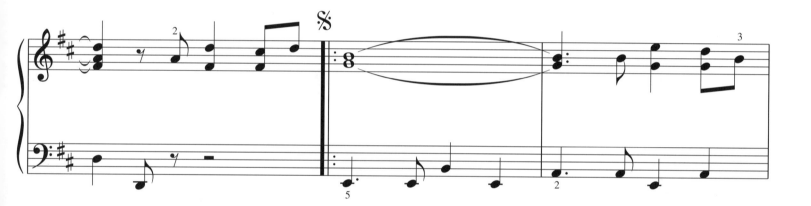

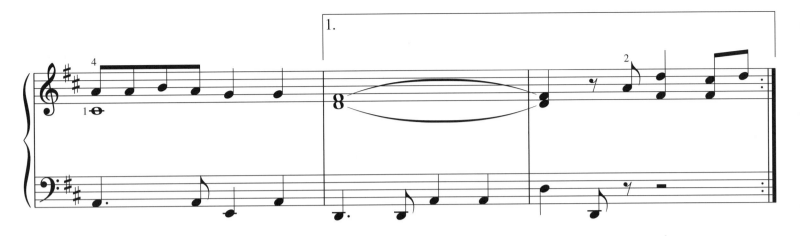

D.S. al Coda
(take 2nd ending)

To Coda $\oplus$

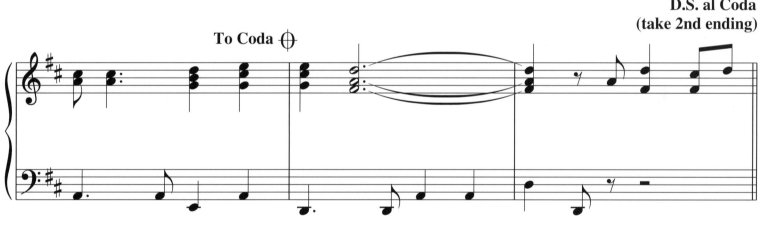

CODA
$\oplus$

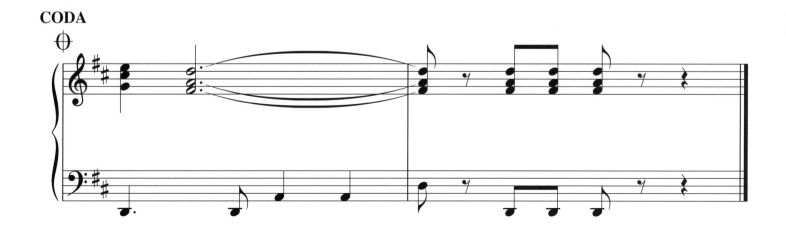

HAPPY HOLIDAY

from the Motion Picture Irving Berlin's HOLIDAY INN

Words and Music by
IRVING BERLIN

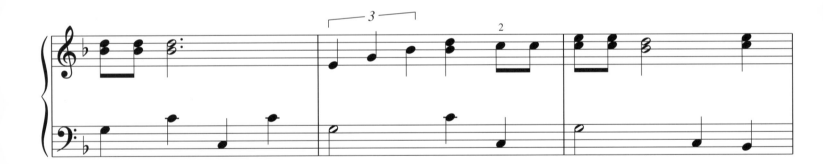

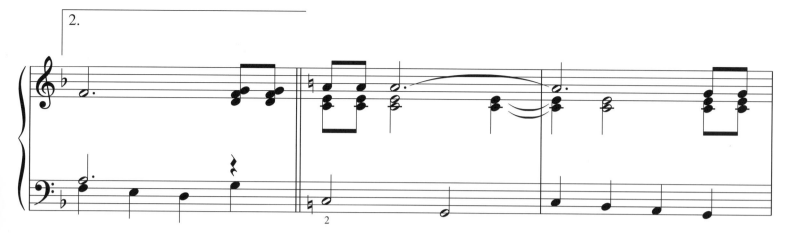

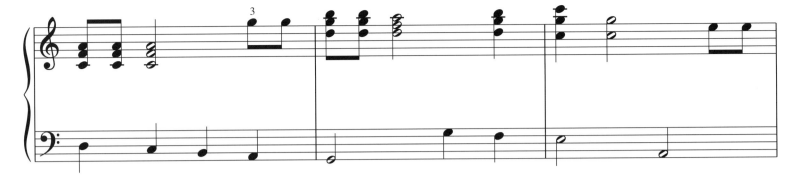

A HOLLY JOLLY CHRISTMAS

Music and Lyrics by
JOHNNY MARKS

Moderately bright, happy

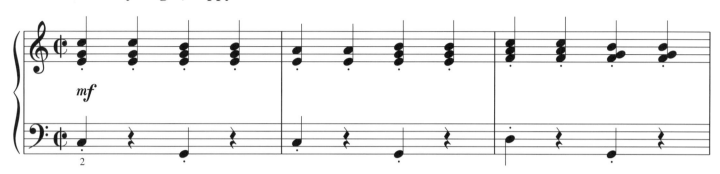

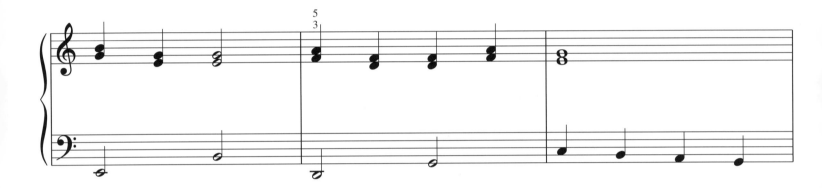

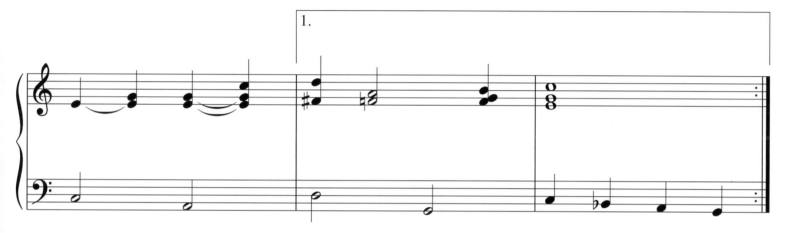

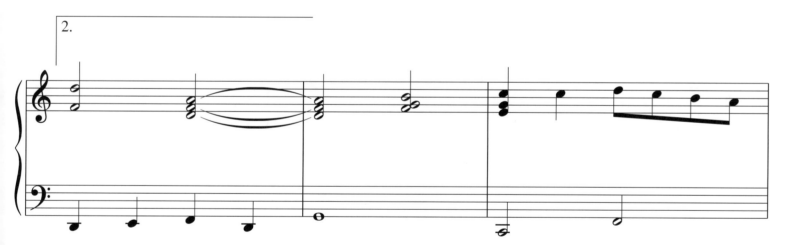

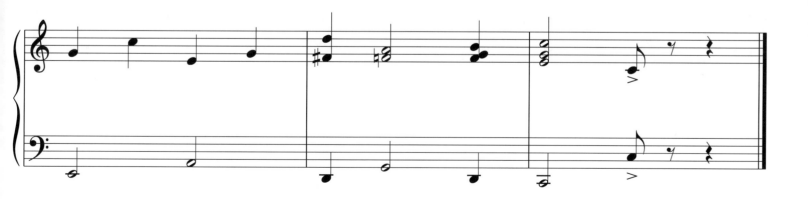

I HEARD THE BELLS ON CHRISTMAS DAY

Words by HENRY LONGFELLOW
Adapted by JOHNNY MARKS
Music by JOHNNY MARKS

Slowly, with expression

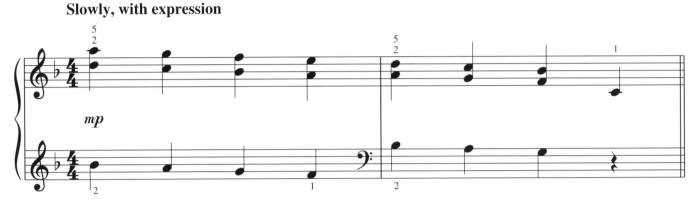

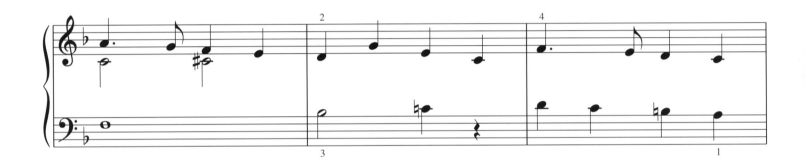

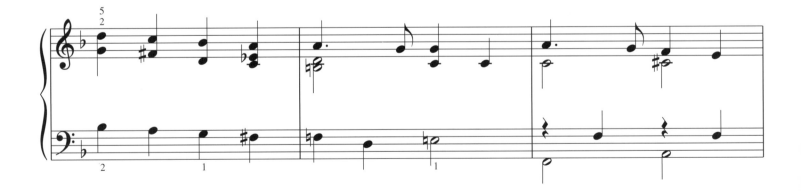

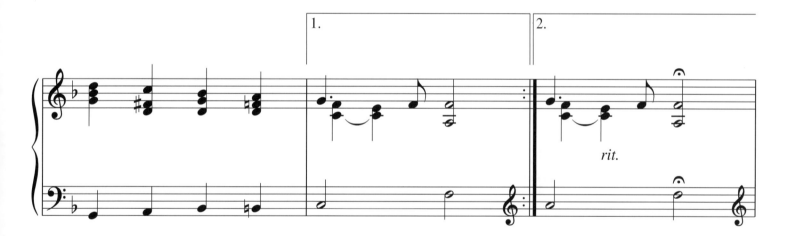

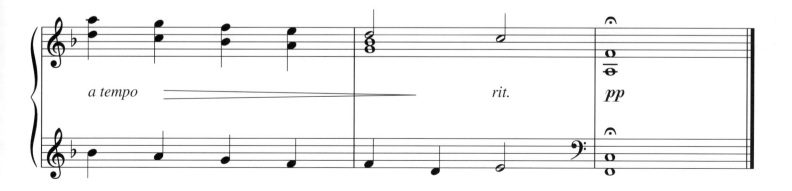

JINGLE-BELL ROCK

Words and Music by JOE BEAL
and JIM BOOTHE

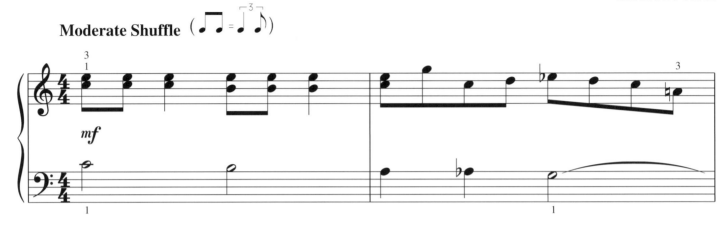

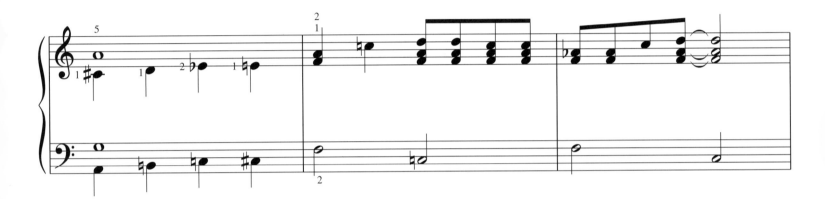

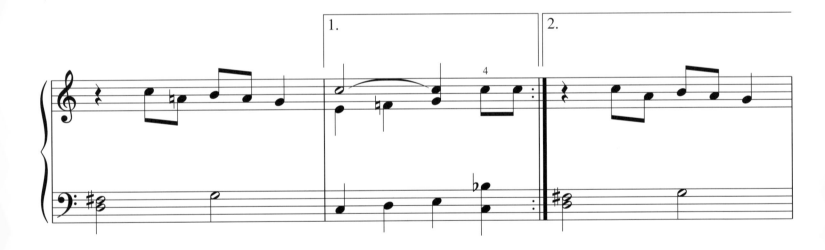

I SAW MOMMY KISSING
SANTA CLAUS

Words and Music by
TOMMIE CONNOR

Moderate Swing

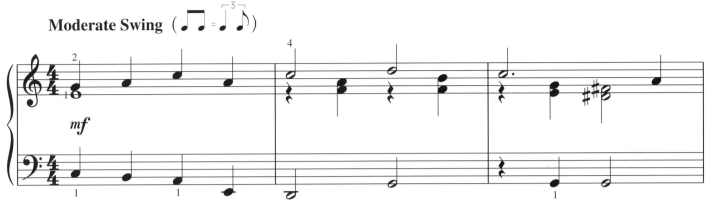

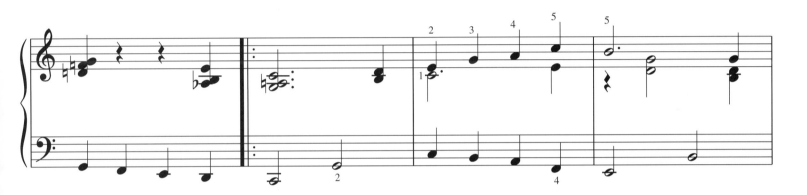

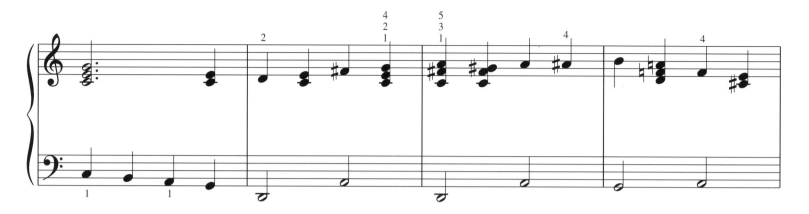

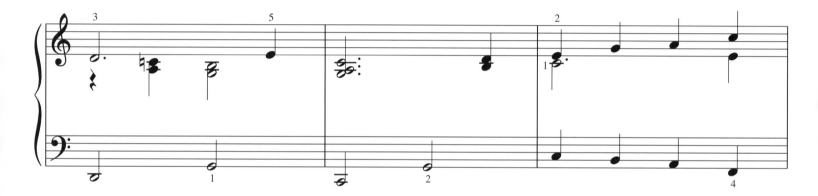

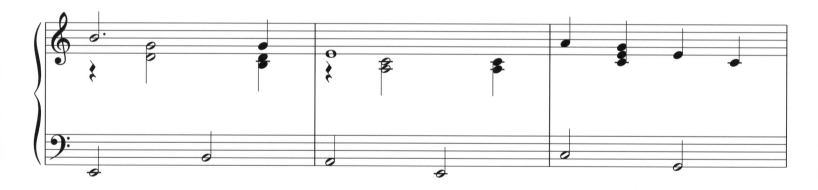

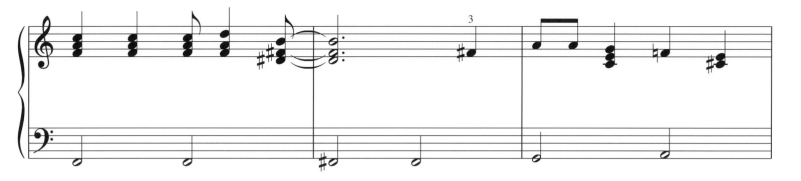

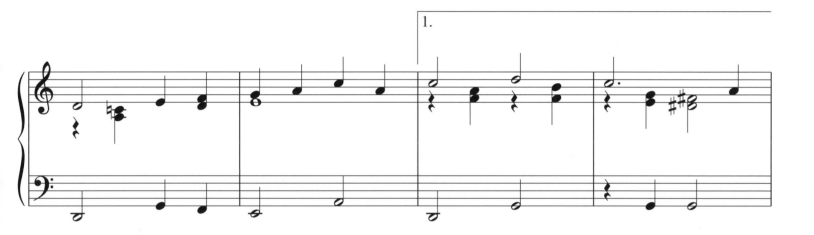

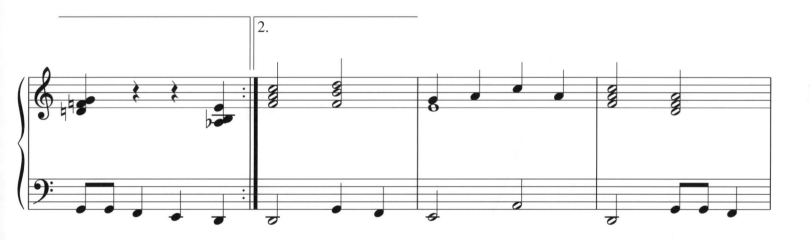

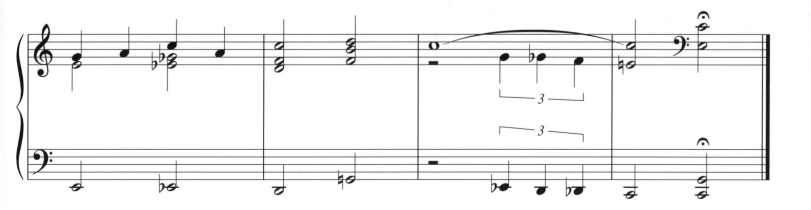

A MARSHMALLOW WORLD

Words by CARL SIGMAN
Music by PETER DeROSE

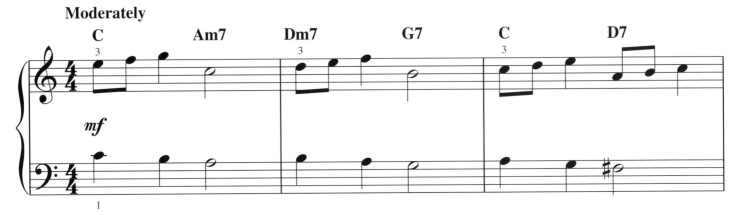

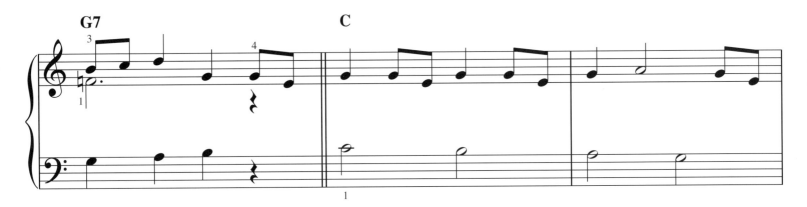

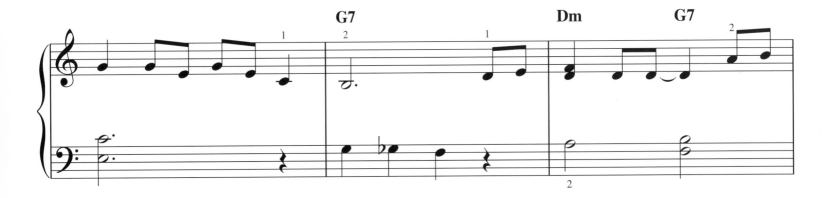

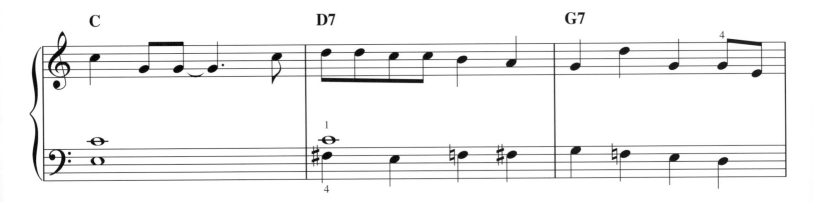

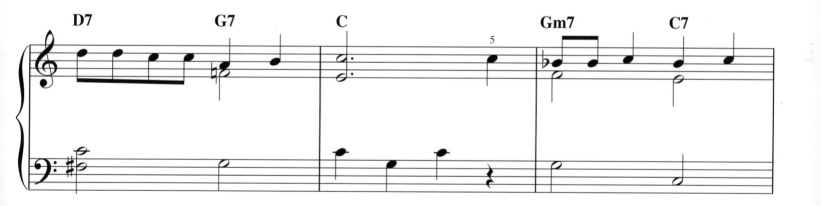

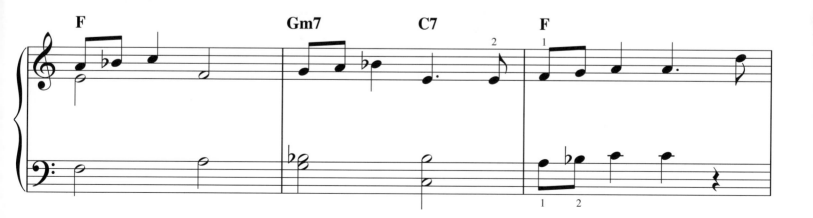

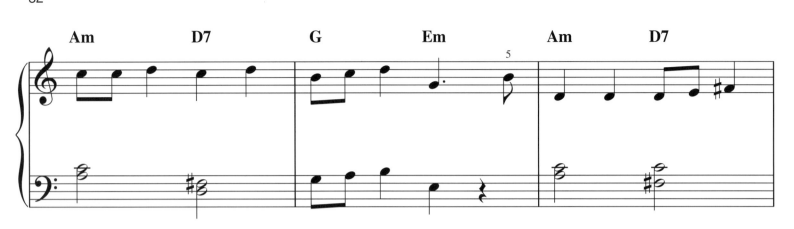

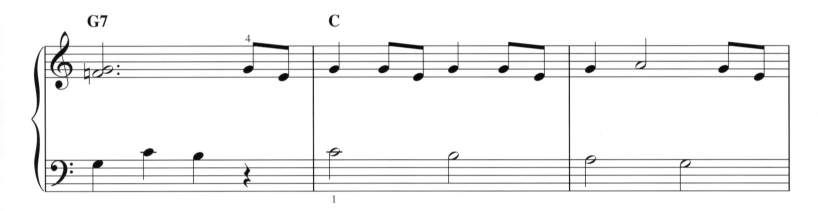

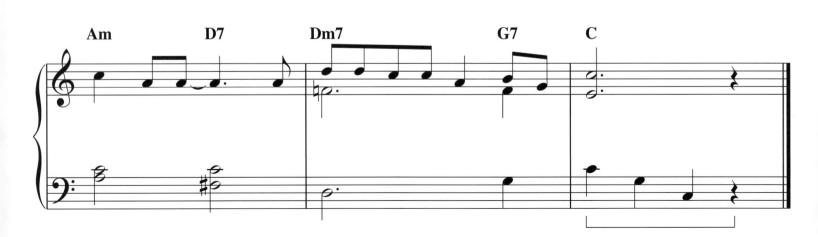

RUDOLPH THE RED-NOSED REINDEER

Music and Lyrics by
JOHNNY MARKS

Freely

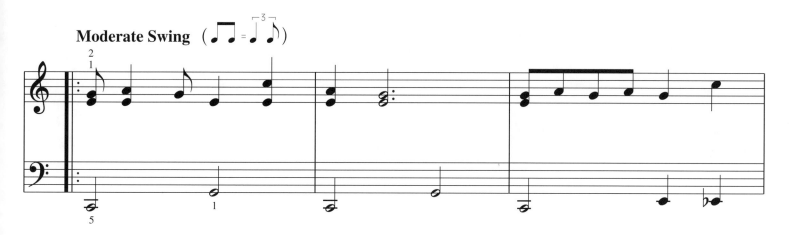

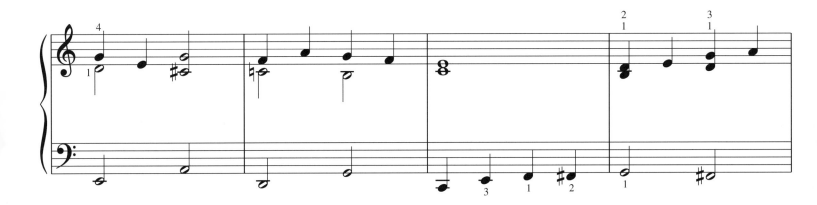

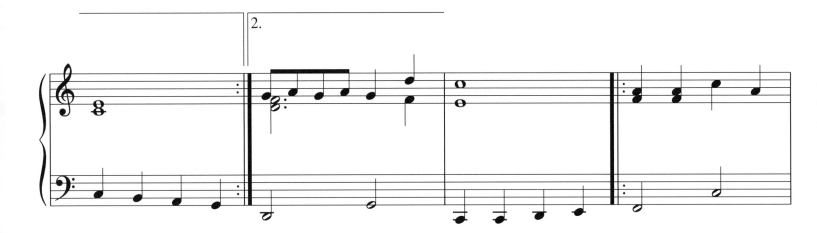

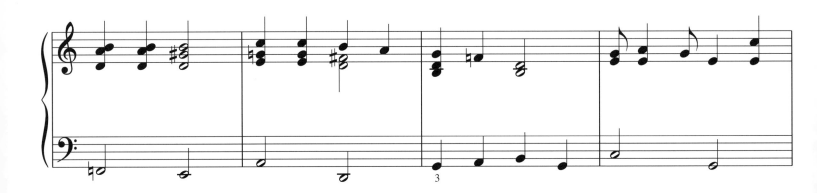

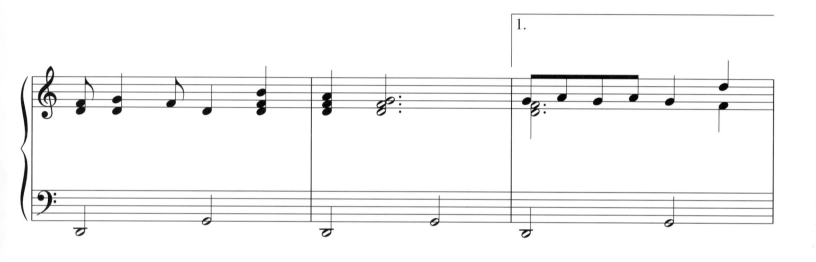

ROCKIN' AROUND
THE CHRISTMAS TREE

Music and Lyrics by
JOHNNY MARKS

Medium Shuffle

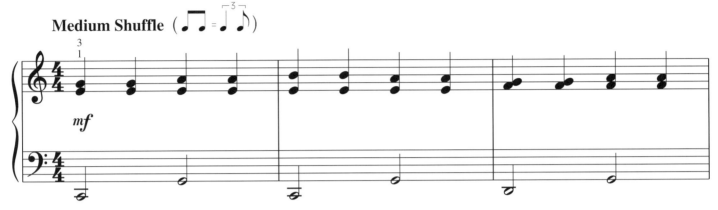

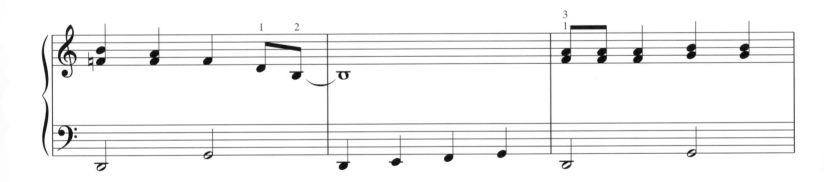

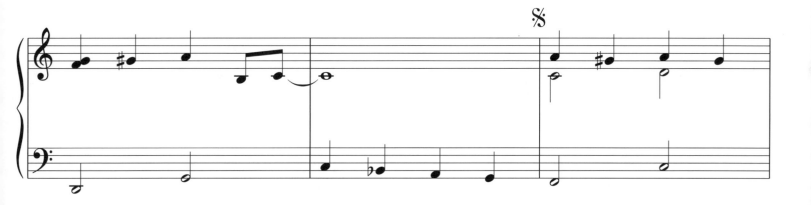

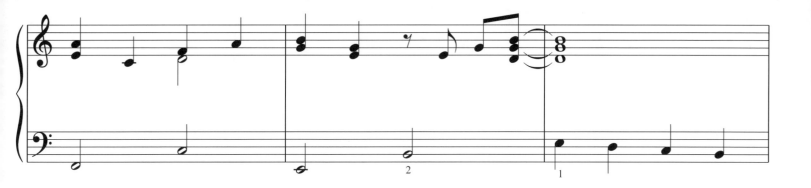

To Coda

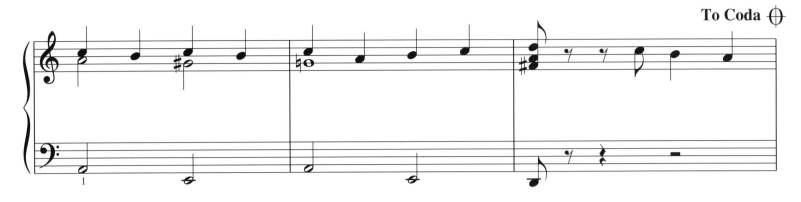

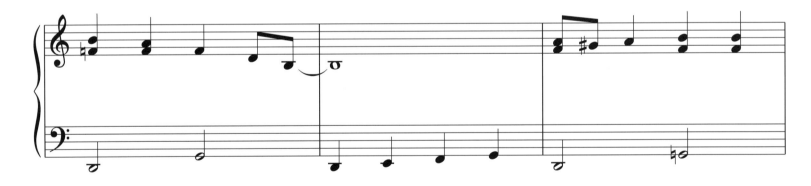

D.S. al Coda

CODA

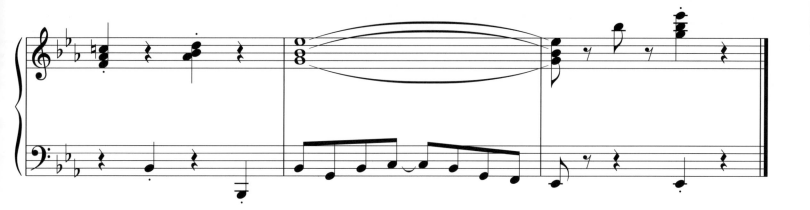

SILVER BELLS
from the Paramount Picture THE LEMON DROP KID

Words and Music by JAY LIVINGSTON
and RAY EVANS

Moderately, with feeling

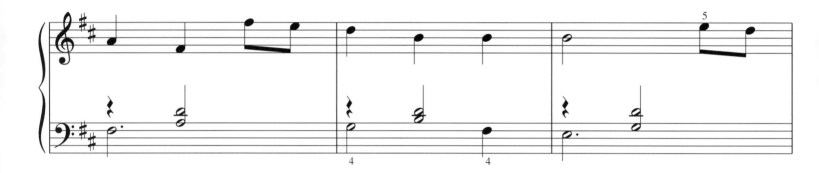

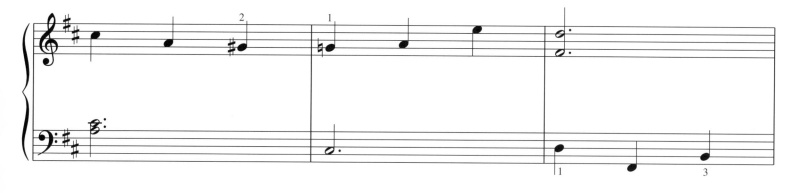

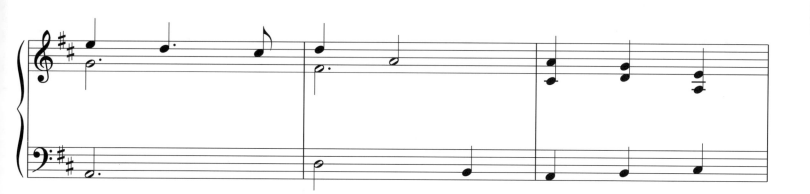

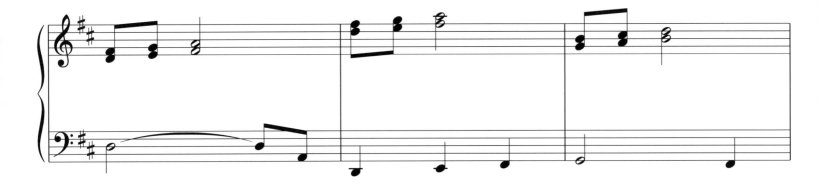

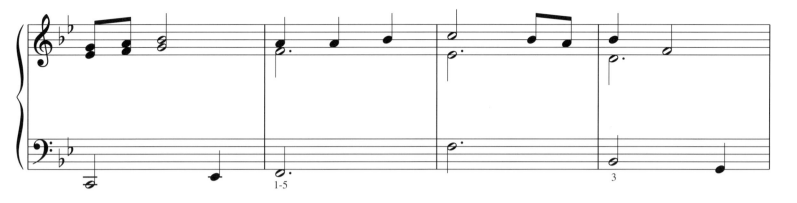

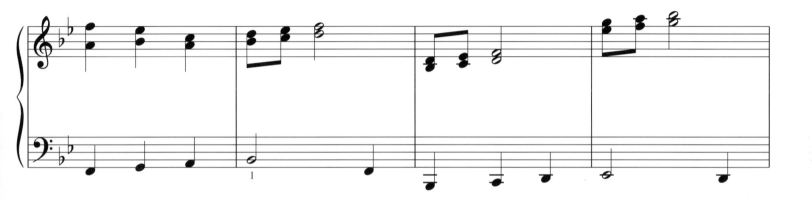

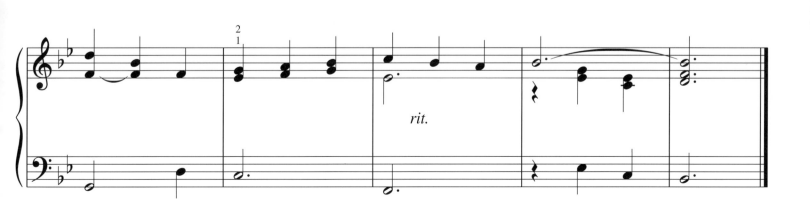

SOMEWHERE IN MY MEMORY

from the Twentieth Century Fox Motion Picture HOME ALONE

Words by LESLIE BRICUSSE
Music by JOHN WILLIAMS

Gently, with simplicity

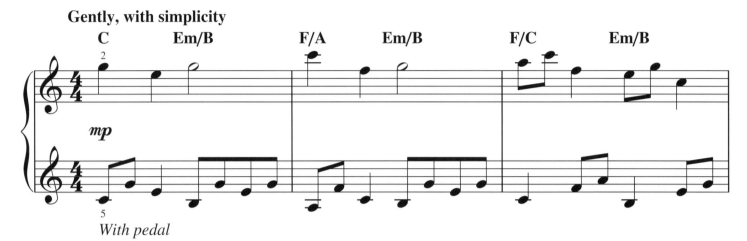

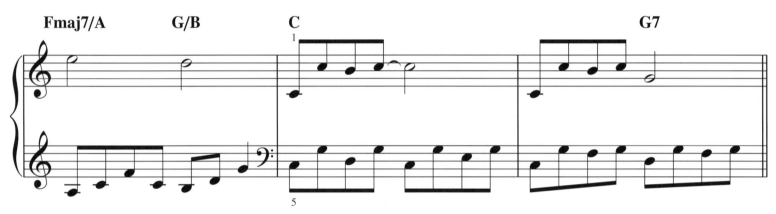

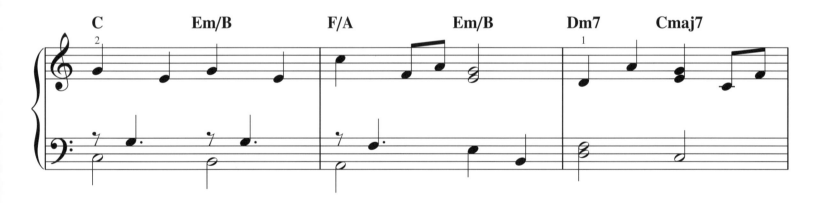

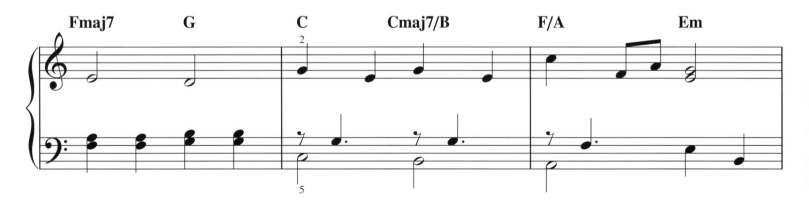

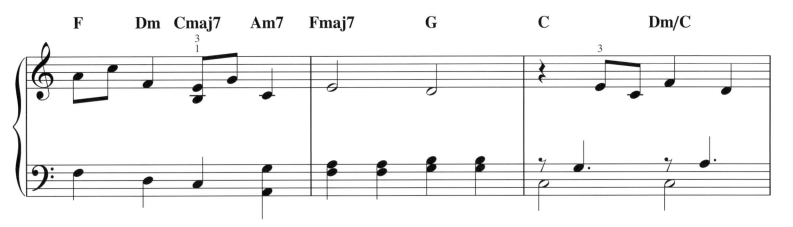

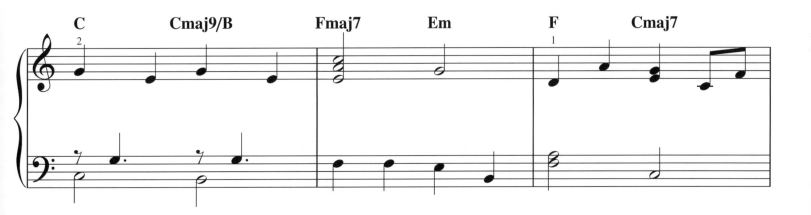

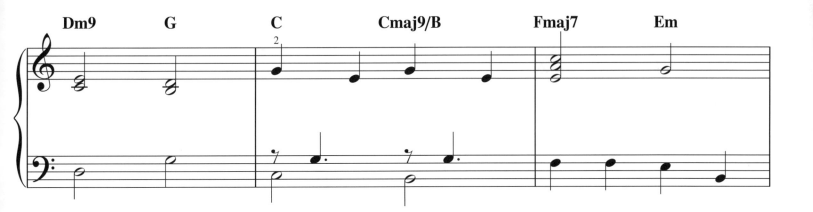

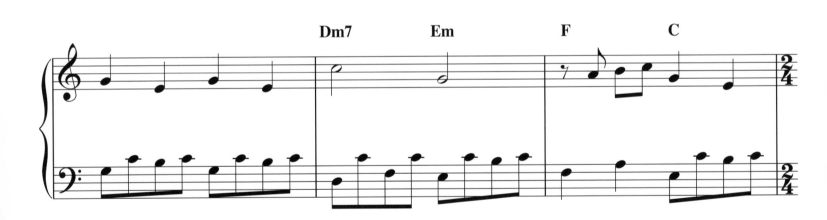

CELEBRATE THE SEASON
with Christmas Songbooks for Piano from Hal Leonard

17 Super Christmas Hits

This book contains the most popular, most requested Christmas titles: The Christmas Song • Frosty the Snow Man • A Holly Jolly Christmas • Home for the Holidays • I'll Be Home for Christmas • It's Beginning to Look like Christmas • Jingle-Bell Rock • Let It Snow! Let It Snow! Let It Snow! • The Little Drummer Boy • Mister Santa • Sleigh Ride • We Need a Little Christmas • and more.
00240867 Big-Note Piano $9.95
00361053 Easy Piano $9.95

25 Top Christmas Songs

Includes: Blue Christmas • C-H-R-I-S-T-M-A-S • The Christmas Song • The Christmas Waltz • Do You Hear What I Hear • Have Yourself a Merry Little Christmas • Here Comes Santa Claus • Jingle-Bell Rock • Last Christmas • Pretty Paper • Silver Bells • and more.
00290064 Big-Note Piano $9.95
00490058 Easy Piano $10.95

Best Christmas Music

A giant collection of 62 Christmas favorites: Away in a Manger • Blue Christmas • The Chipmunk Song • The First Noel • Frosty the Snow Man • Grandma Got Run Over by a Reindeer • I Saw Mommy Kissing Santa Claus • Pretty Paper • Silver Bells • Wonderful Christmastime • more.
00310325 Big-Note Piano $14.95

The Best Christmas Songs Ever

A treasured collection of 70 songs: The Christmas Song • Frosty the Snow Man • Grandma Got Run Over by a Reindeer • Here Comes Santa Claus • A Holly Jolly Christmas • I'll Be Home for Christmas • Jingle-Bell Rock • Let It Snow! Let It Snow! Let It Snow! • Santa Claus Is Comin' to Town • more!
00364130 Easy Piano $18.95

Children's Christmas Songs

22 holiday favorites, including: Frosty the Snow Man • Jingle Bells • Jolly Old St. Nicholas • Rudolph, the Red-Nosed Reindeer • Up on the Housetop • and more!
00222547 Easy Piano $7.95

Christmas Pops
THE PHILLIP KEVEREN SERIES

18 holiday favorites: Because It's Christmas • Blue Christmas • Christmas Time Is Here • I'll Be Home for Christmas • Mary, Did You Know? • Rockin' Around the Christmas Tree • Silver Bells • Tennessee Christmas • more.
00311126 Easy Piano $12.95

Christmas Songs

12 songs, including: Caroling, Caroling • Christmas Time Is Here • Do You Hear What I Hear • Here Comes Santa Claus • It's Beginning to Look like Christmas • Little Saint Nick • Merry Christmas, Darling • Mistletoe and Holly • and more.
00311242 Easy Piano Solo....................................$8.95

Christmas Traditions
THE PHILLIP KEVEREN SERIES

20 beloved songs arranged for beginning soloists: Away in a Manger • Coventry Carol • Deck the Hall • God Rest Ye Merry, Gentlemen • Jingle Bells • Silent Night • We Three Kings of Orient Are • more.
00311117 Beginning Piano Solos................................$9.95

Greatest Christmas Hits

18 Christmas classics: Blue Christmas • Brazilian Sleigh Bells • The Christmas Song • Do You Hear What I Hear • Here Comes Santa Claus • I Saw Mommy Kissing Santa Claus • Silver Bells • This Christmas • more!
00311136 Big-Note Piano $9.95

Jazz Up Your Christmas
ARRANGED BY LEE EVANS

12 Christmas carols in a fresh perspective. Full arrangements may be played as a concert suite. Songs include: Deck the Hall • The First Noel • God Rest Ye Merry Gentlemen • The Holly and the Ivy • O Christmas Tree • What Child Is This? • and more.
00009040 Piano Solo $7.95

Jingle Jazz
THE PHILLIP KEVEREN SERIES

17 Christmas standards: Caroling, Caroling • The Christmas Song • I'll Be Home for Christmas • Jingle Bells • Merry Christmas, Darling • The Most Wonderful Time of the Year • Rudolph the Red-Nosed Reindeer • We Wish You a Merry Christmas • and more.
00310762 Piano Solo $12.95

100 Christmas Carols

Includes the Christmas classics: Angels We Have Heard on High • Bring a Torch, Jeannette Isabella • Dance of the Sugar Plum Fairy • The First Noel • Here We Come A-Wassailing • It Came upon the Midnight Clear • Joy to the World • Still, Still, Still • The Twelve Days of Christmas • We Three Kings of Orient Are • and more!
00311134 Easy Piano $14.95

The Nutcracker Suite
ARRANGED BY BILL BOYD

7 easy piano arrangements from Tchaikovsky's beloved ballet. Includes "Dance of the Sugar-Plum Fairy."
00110010 Easy Piano $8.95

The Ultimate Series: Christmas

The ultimate collection of Christmas classics includes 100 songs: Carol of the Bells • The Chipmunk Song • Christmas Time Is Here • Do You Hear What I Hear • The First Noel • Gesù Bambino • Happy Xmas (War Is Over) • Jesu, Joy of Man's Desiring • Silver and Gold • What Child Is This? • Wonderful Christmastime • and more.
00241003 Easy Piano $19.95

FOR MORE INFORMATION, SEE YOUR LOCAL MUSIC DEALER, OR WRITE TO:

HAL•LEONARD® CORPORATION
7777 W. BLUEMOUND RD. P.O. BOX 13819 MILWAUKEE, WI 53213
Complete songlists online at **www.halleonard.com**

Prices, contents and availability subject to change without notice.

0606

The Greatest Songs Ever Written

The Best Ever Collection

Arranged for Easy Piano with Lyrics.

The Best Broadway Songs Ever

66 songs: All I Ask of You • Cabaret • Comedy Tonight • Don't Cry for Me Argentina • Getting to Know You • If I Were a Rich Man • Memory • Ol' Man River • People • Younger Than Springtime • and many more!
00300178 ....$19.95

The Best Children's Songs Ever

102 songs: Alphabet Song • The Ballad of Davy Crockett • Bingo • A Dream Is a Wish Your Heart Makes • Eensy Weensy Spider • The Farmer in the Dell • Frere Jacques • Hello Mudduh, Hello Fadduh! • I'm Popeye the Sailor Man • Jesus Loves Me • The Muffin Man • On Top of Spaghetti • Puff the Magic Dragon • A Spoonful of Sugar • Twinkle, Twinkle Little Star • Winnie the Pooh • and more.
00310360 ....$19.95

The Best Christmas Songs Ever

69 of the most-loved songs of the season: Auld Lang Syne • Blue Christmas • The Christmas Song (Chestnuts Roasting on an Open Fire) • Feliz Navidad • Grandma Got Run Over by a Reindeer • Happy Xmas (War Is Over) • I'll Be Home for Christmas • Jingle-Bell Rock • Let It Snow! Let It Snow! Let It Snow! • My Favorite Things • Old Toy Trains • Rudolph, The Red-Nosed Reindeer • Santa Claus is Comin' to Town • Toyland • You're All I Want for Christmas • and more.
00364130 ....$18.95

The Best Contemporary Christian Songs Ever

50 songs: Awesome God • The Basics of Life • Can't Live a Day • Ed Shaddai • Father's Eyes • Great Is the Lord • His Strength Is Perfect • I Can Only Imagine • Jesus Will Still Be There • Lamb of God • Oh Lord, You're Beautiful • Place in This World • Steady On • This Is Your Time • Via Dolorosa • We Can Make a Difference • and more.
00311069 ....$18.95

The Best Country Songs Ever

78 songs, featuring: Always on My Mind • Could I Have This Dance • Crazy • Daddy Sang Bass • Forever and Ever, Amen • God Bless the U.S.A. • I Fall to Pieces • Jambalaya • King of the Road • Love Without End, Amen • Mammas, Don't Let Your Babies Grow Up to Be Cowboys • Paper Roses • Rocky Top • Sixteen Tons • Through the Years • Your Cheatin' Heart • and more.
00311540 ....$17.95

The Best Easy Listening Songs Ever

75 songs: And I Love You So • Blue Velvet • Candle on the Water • Do You Know the Way to San Jose • Don't Cry Out Loud • Feelings • The Girl from Ipanema • Hey Jude • I Write the Songs • Just Once • Love Takes Time • Make the World Go Away • Nadia's Theme • One Voice • The Rainbow Connection • Sailing • Through the Years • Unchained Melody • Vincent (Starry Starry Night) • We've Only Just Begun • You Are So Beautiful • and more.
00311119 ....$17.95

The Best Gospel Songs Ever

74 gospel songs, including: Amazing Grace • Blessed Assurance • Do Lord • Give Me That Old Time Religion • How Great Thou Art • I'll Fly Away • Just a Closer Walk with Thee • More Than Wonderful • The Old Rugged Cross • Precious Lord, Take My Hand (Take My Hand, Precious Lord) • Turn Your Radio On • The Unclouded Day • When the Roll Is Called up Yonder • Will the Circle Be Unbroken • and many more.
00310781 ....$19.95

The Best Hymns Ever

116 hymns: Amazing Grace • Beneath the Cross of Jesus • Christ the Lord Is Risen Today • Down by the Riverside • For the Beauty of the Earth • Holy, Holy, Holy • It Is Well with My Soul • Joyful, Joyful We Adore Thee • Let Us Break Bread Together • A Mighty Fortress Is Our God • The Old Rugged Cross • Rock of Ages • Were You There? • and more.
00311120 ....$17.95

The Best Jazz Standards Ever

71 jazzy tunes: Ain't Misbehavin' • Bye Bye Blackbird • Don't Get Around Much Anymore • Easy to Love • The Girl from Ipanema • It Don't Mean a Thing (If It Ain't Got That Swing) • The Lady Is a Tramp • My Funny Valentine • The Nearness of You • Old Devil Moon • Satin Doll • Stardust • Tangerine • and more.
00311091 ....$17.95

The Best Love Songs Ever

65 favorite love songs: Always • Beautiful in My Eyes • Can You Feel the Love Tonight • Endless Love • Feelings • Have I Told You Lately • Isn't It Romantic? • Just the Way You Are • Longer • My Funny Valentine • Saving All My Love for You • Vision of Love • When I Fall in Love • Your Song • and more.
00310128 ....$17.95

The Best Movie Songs Ever

71 songs: Alfie • Beauty and the Beast • Born Free • Circle of Life • Endless Love • Theme from *Jaws* • Moon River • Somewhere Out There • Speak Softly, Love • Take My Breath Away • Unchained Melody • A Whole New World • and more.
00310141 ....$19.95

The Best Praise & Worship Songs Ever

74 songs: Agnus Dei • Better Is One Day • Come, Now Is the Time to Worship • Days of Elijah • Firm Foundation • God of Wonders • Here I Am to Worship • I Can Only Imagine • Jesus, Lover of My Soul • Lamb of God • More Precious Than Silver • Open the Eyes of My Heart • Shine, Jesus, Shine • There Is a Redeemer • We Bow Down • You Are My King (Amazing Love) • and more.
00311312 ....$17.95

The Best Rock Songs Ever

More than 60 favorites: All Shook Up • Born to Be Wild • California Dreamin' • Duke of Earl • Free Bird • Great Balls of Fire • Hey Jude • I Love Rock 'N Roll • Imagine • Let It Be • My Generation • Na Na Hey Hey Kiss Him Goodbye • Oh, Pretty Woman • Rock Around the Clock • Spinning Wheel • Takin' Care of Business • Under the Boardwalk • Wild Thing • and more.
00310444 ....$17.95

The Best Songs Ever

71 must-own classics: All I Ask of You • Blue Skies • Call Me Irresponsible • Crazy • Edelweiss • Georgia on My Mind • Imagine • Love Me Tender • Moonlight in Vermont • My Funny Valentine • Piano Man • Satin Doll • Tears in Heaven • Unforgettable • The Way We Were • When I Fall in Love • and more.
00359223 ....$19.95

More of the Best Songs Ever

72 more classic songs: Alfie • Beyond the Sea • Come Rain or Come Shine • Don't Know Why • Every Breath You Take • The Glory of Love • Heart and Soul • In the Mood • Michelle • My Cherie Amour • The Nearness of You • One • Respect • Stand By Me • Take the "A" Train • Up Where We Belong • What'll I Do? • Young at Heart • and more.
00311090 ....$19.95

FOR MORE INFORMATION, SEE YOUR LOCAL MUSIC DEALER, OR WRITE TO:

HAL•LEONARD®
CORPORATION
7777 W. BLUEMOUND RD. P.O. BOX 13819 MILWAUKEE, WI 53213
www.halleonard.com

Prices, contents, and availability subject to change without notice. Not all products available outside the U.S.A.

0707